LOVE PAIN & RECOVERY
THE POETIC EXPERIENCE:
VOLUME I

LOVE PAIN & RECOVERY

The Poetic Experience: Volume I

EVANS A. BROWN
Author

Published by Imagiread

Copyright © 2012 by Evans A. Brown

All rights are reserved. No part of this publication may be reproduced, stored in a retrieval system, or transmitted in any form or by any means, electronic, mechanical, photocopying, recording, or otherwise, without prior permission of the publishing company.

Identifiers:
ISBN 978-0-9850268-9-9
PRINT ISBN 978-1-7355250-7-5

First Printing, 2022

ACKNOWLEDGEMENT

I recognize the greatness of the people in my life. I would like to thank my mother for her strength and my sister for all of her prayers. My cousins Dina and Niecie for always being there for me. My Aunts' Lo and Zell for their LOVE and my best friends, Eric Alva, and his wife for never turning their backs on me.

I also need to thank my neighbor and sister DeDe for reminding me of my faith as well as some of my true friends. They include Harry H.,Veniecia C.,Clarence W., Cheryl, Reggie A., Smooth, John B., Kenny Mc., Damon B., Ms. Amber Eddie W., Emilio, Derek Erwin, and my sponsor, Dathan for being a friend and brother.

I need to say a special THANK YOU to "The Group" for helping me to realize that life is best lived outside of the box. To all of my loved ones that have carried on, most especially my grandmothers, my daddy, my brother, and uncles for their strength and memories,

Thank you!

FOREWORD

by Dina Williams

I have the fondest memories of Evans and I as young children. I think about all of the good times we had at church, school and of course, home. That home for both of us meant being reared in an environment of unconditional LOVE and one that encouraged us to be proud of who we were and would someday become. For me that would mean I would become an educator and for Evans that meant he would become a professional baseball player.

When Evans set out to follow that dream, our family was very proud of his accomplishments. As time passed however, Evans found himself facing distractions left and right. As a result of those distractions he would learn the greatest of strengths through his weaknesses and eventually came to experience heart wrenching PAIN. I look back on some of his struggles and see how many reminded him that they had "told him so" but I remained supportive of him even in the midst of him slipping completely away.

After being repeatedly incarcerated for over a decade, experiencing broken relationships and bouts of self-discovery, Evans finally decided that he had hurt enough.

How does one go from LOVE to PAIN to RECOVERY? It wasn't easy but with perseverance I witnessed Evans endure with his answer being "one day at a time". I am proud to say that my cousin is indeed restored and that he is and will always be.

PART I

Let us being with love

You fill my life

You fill my life with laughter
You fill my heart with joy
You fill my life with many things
Things I can't ignore
You fill my life with happiness
And this no one can replace
You fill my life with a smile
A smile that can't be erased
You fill my life with sunshine
That always warms my face
You fill my life with joyful behaviors
At times I believe you are a savior

Intoxicating Love

From the first time I saw you
It came to my mind
Intoxicating love had been
So hard to find
One look in your eyes
This love I could feel
Intoxicating love
Yours had to be real
Intoxicating love
Its now and forever
Intoxicating love
Shall keep us together

Think of Me

Think of me at the start of your day
With these thoughts you'll be on your way
Think of me if you start to cry
Think of me when there's no one there
With these thought my love will care
Think of me when you have fears
With these thoughts I'm still real near
Think of me when you are feeling sad
With these thoughts you'll be real glad
Think of me when you feel frustrated
Think of me just because you can
Think of me

GOD WILL

God will provide for you
When everything seems lost
God will provide for you
It's just a little cost
God will provide for you
When there's no one there
God will provide for you
Just say a little prayer
God will provide for you
When you can't call a friend
God will provide for you
And he will be there in the end

YOU ARE

You are the apple of my eye
The sunshine that brightens my day
You are the thought that guides my way
The joy that fills my heart
You are my motivation from the start
The one which makes me smile
You are so special to be around
The one who lifts me when I'm down
You are the one whom eyes I see
And you are my most beautiful rose

Forever

Forever is a long long time
Some call it everlasting
Forever is a long long time
But that's how long you should be mine
Forever is a long long time
Forever I want to love you still
Forever is a long long time
Now is it God's will
Forever is a long long time
Can you see forever
Forever is a long long time
And trust our love and our togetherness
Forever is a long long time
Can you say forever

Daddy

*Daddy was a great man
With hands made of stone
The sound of his voice would
Cut right through your heart and soul
Daddy was loved by everyone
And never meant no harm
Daddy I miss you right now today
And still feel the embrace of your arms
Your presence is felt right today
And I'll see you one day
I'm heaven bound Daddy
And thanks for the time
You were around*

She's Like

She's like an Angel who is sent from above
And she always has that unconditional love
She's like a savior with so much faith
And will lift your spirits when most others can't
For she's like a flower that blooms in the seasons
And will touch your heart for all the right reasons
She's like a teacher and some days she preaches
And each word she speaks you must believe it
She's like no other you've ever known
And if she's too far just pick up the phone
She is a mother who was placed on the earth
And you can't put value on what a mother is worth

Beautiful

Like a rainbow after the rain falls
Like the sunset on a winter day
Like the moonlight that shines at night
Like the sunshine on a lovely day
Like the birth of a man born child
Like the flowers that bloom in spring
Like a mocking bird when it sings
Beautiful you are, beautiful

A Welcome Sight

A Welcome Sight
This is all you need to be
You mean so much, you really do
Now can you really see
A welcome sight you are to me
I pray each day to thee
To keep you safe, to win this race
You keep my heart in place
A welcome sight you are to me
Is this our final test
To live together forever and ever
And prove our love is best
A welcome sight you are to me
Let's stand upon the stage
And raise our arms to all
Of those who thought
It couldn't be done
A welcome sight you are to me

Anything You Want
Anything You Can Have

Anything you want
Anything you can have
All that I possess
Now I must confess
Loving one another
We have never lost
Togetherness which keeps us
Oh so very close
Smiles and the laughter so often that we share
Caring for each other this we must declare
A guiding force within us
Which guides us through the day
Our joy and pain allows us to look this way
The conversations we share

The words we say
Understanding each other
In a way no one can
A fulfillment which fills the gaps
This is who we are
Our beauty from within
Automatically we win
Thoughts and our visions
Will let the world know
Dreams that we have
Keeps us wanting more
Because a love like this has never been before
Anything you want
Anything you can have

Beautiful (Happy Mother's Day)

Like a church that's full of praise
And a baby when its raised
Like the flowers that bloom in the spring
And a rainbow after it rains
Like the sunset on a summer night
And with it that spiritual light
Like the love from one mother
You know there's no other
Beautiful you are
Beautiful

Love Unlimited

Love Unlimited is not a fantasy
Or an imagination in your mind
It's a love of understanding
A feeling that's deep inside
So unbelievable you can't hide
A vision for all to see
Look in the mirror see what you see
Deep in your soul it means so much
Caring and sharing with a gentle touch
The knowledge of what love is about
All you can do is keep it in your thought
And tell the whole world you have found
Love unlimited

I Found Heaven in You

I've never been to heaven only dreamed of it
Incredible and remarkable, I found heaven in you
From the moment we held hands and that minute that we kissed
I knew then heaven I had not missed
Everything was so natural in love came to mind
Heaven I found in you, you're one of a kind
You have made me understand unspeakable joy
So elated each day I want to love you more
Always stay as you are please never change
More beautiful than a flower you keep me amazed How could this be a dream with all that I feel Reality is what it is now I must believe
The peace within your heart that you gave to me The assurance which you have the honesty I see Your blessings from above has turned into love

Each night on my knees I always pray to thee
I've never been to heaven only dreamed of it
Incredible and remarkable I found heaven in you

Let me be the one

Let me be the one to hold you in the night
Let me be the one to make everything right
Let me be the one to whisper in your ear
Let me be the one to dry your every tear
Let me be the one to hold you in my arms
Let me be the one to fill you with charm
Let me be the one you can call your own
Let me be the one to love you forever more
Just let me be the one that you always look for

LOVE

Love is something that is shared
And in our life we need
Love is something that will put
A smile back on your face
Love is something that is real
And is wonderful to feel
Love is something that when you find it
You will know the deal

Mesmerized

You captured me with your beauty
Mesmerized me with your smile
Fulfilled me with some love
Which came from within your heart
Amazing was your touch
How could I be in a rush
Dazzling like the sunset
And more gentle as a lamb
You have made me who I am
And the perfect match we are
Our love is here to stay
No other can take that away
With every fiber of my being
Together love has brought new meaning
Thank you for entering my life

For without you how could I see
Today you have made me
Understand who I need to be
You captured me with your beauty
And mesmerized me with your smile

More Beautiful

More beautiful than you realize
Because your eyes may not see
More beautiful than you realize
And all you mean to me
More beautiful that you realize
But maybe you can understand
More beautiful than you realize
And how you are part of God's plan
More beautiful than you realize
Can I hold you tonight
More beautiful than you realize
Yes you are my guiding light

Mother's Day

Mother's day is everyday
Not just a day in May
For Mother's all over the world
Are greater than diamonds and pearls
For each mother has a specialty
And mine might differ from yours
Best rest assure that all mothers
Are the best in all the world

My Most Beautiful Rose

My most beautiful rose is special every way
Her touch, her smile, her smell, her walk will bring joy everyday
My most beautiful rose is one of the trust
No fuss, no rush, no hush
My most beautiful rose is willing to give
In my life I live
My most beautiful rose is one of beauty
She always knows what she is doing
My most beautiful rose is one that cares
And in my life she is always there
My most beautiful rose is a lady
And I'm crazy about my most beautiful rose

Thank you Mom

*Thank you mom for all you've done
Thank you mom it's been a long run
Thank you mom for being so real
Thank you mom, I know how you feel
Thank you mom for teaching me right
Thank you mom for your spiritual light
Thank you mom for all your strength
Thank you mom for all your sense
Thank you mom for all my dreams
Thank you mom, that's what I scream*

Seems Like

Seems like only yesterday
An Angel came my way
A smile and demeanor a thousand words can't say Beauty which came from within you had to be heaven sent
Our hearts began to beat as one today I convinced As I gazed into your eyes I started to realize
The special meaning within God has sent my prize No other had ever touched me the way you had With you as part of my life how could I be sad
How I long to hold you close all through the day For thoughts of you lift me up when my days seem gray
On my knees at night I pray to be who you need me to be
GOD sent me an Angel
An Angel to be with me

My Destiny

*Can I hold you close to me
So the world can see
Will you allow me to explain
The man I used to be
Can I experience life with you
The ups and downs we may go through
Let me interest you in some love
That's the only heaven sent
Can I whisper in your ear
Tonight and all year
And help you understand
All that I have planned
Can I tell you my dreams
And things that are in my heart*

Let you know how much
I have loved you from the start
Can I capture your mind
Yes it is our time
And walk together hand in hand
Because you are my destiny

True Friend

Friendship is a priceless gift
That cannot be bought nor sold
For its value is far greater
Than a mountain made of gold
For gold is cold and lifeless
It can neither hear nor see
And in your time of trouble
It is powerless to cheer
So when God does not
Send you diamonds, rings or pearls
Be thankful that he sends
Love from a true friend

Your Eyes

Each day I rise and late at night
It's your eyes I must see
Because when I look into your eyes
I began to realize things I could not see
Like the emotion of your heart
That makes me who I am today
The devotion, focus and love
That swept me off my feet
No other has ever touched me In a way which you have
When I first looked into your eyes
Love is all I felt
Don't allow others to fill your mind
With things they don't know
Understand that I love you
And forever I have been true
Now jealousy an enemy
But in love we glow
Each day I rise and late at night
It's your eyes I must see

When I think of You

When I think of you the world stops turning
And you become my world
When I think of you I feel good all over
Because your love is a panacea for all my ills
When I think of you I think of GOD and thank
him For blessing me with a wonderful woman like
you When I think of you I smile
Because you give me unspeakable joy
When I think of you I think of us
Because we will always be as one
When I think of you I wish the day had more hours
So I could love you just a little bit more
Take care my love
While I think of you

The Reason

*You are the reason I woke up this morning with
a smile on my face
You are the reason my heart
stays in the right place
You are the reason when the sun came up and the
birds began to sing
You are the reason the roses bloom
so early in the spring you are the reason
God placed that rainbow after the rain
You are the reason today my life is really not that
strange
You are the reason in my life
I have no worries you are the reason in my walk
I have so much glory
You are the reason that love comes from the heavens
above*

You are the reason that GOD made a boy and a girl You are the reason for all seasons so I tell you once again
you are the reason and I will always love you to the very end because
You are the reason

PART II

Sometimes leads to Pain

For Real

For Real is the pain I feel
For Real is my only will
For Real are those days gone by
For Real are my reasons why
For Real Lord just show me how
For Real is this time right now
For Real is that inner peace
For Real is what I seek
For Real is this man to be
For Real is my freedom you see
For Real is the lord of all
For Real is Jesus standing tall
For Real just believe you see
The ultimate person you can be

Everything in You

Today I'm lost and need to find you
Because my soul is empty
Over and over I've wronged you
I know there's been plenty
Now I'm here to say I'm different
I've changed for the good
You probably can't believe me
Maybe you thought I never would
My soul is broken down
Without you in my life
Breaking up was so sudden
We did not think twice
There's a hole in my heart
That's really hard to close
People say you don't know what you
have until that love is gone

My heart is heavy
Today I'm all alone
I miss your face and your smile
I know it's been awhile
Most of all I miss living because I
have nothing in me and
Everything in You

Yesterday was really bad
Today almost too much
I miss your warm embrace
And the way you used to blush
I took our love for granted
I truly need you back
I'm fighting for you everyday
There's nothing but truth in that
All this time has come and gone
Since I've seen your face
Each night I pray to God
No other has taken my place
I need you more than life itself
To bring me through this gray
Deep inside my heart
I pray you feel the same way
So kiss my face and touch my lips
And allow our love to shine
And please understand I miss living
Because I have nothing in me and
Everything in You

Brother

Brother you are truly missed
And my life has been a mess
Now I've changed my way of thinking And I know I'm truly blessed
I felt the pain when you left
And still feel it today
Just know when I placed you in that ground
I knew you were heaven bound

God's Children

When will the madness stop
How does the pain go away
How does the sadness end
When will the happiness begin
Can we live our life in a positive
way Will the light of God
Ever shine our way
How will we prosper and persevere
Can we learn to ease the fears within
In God we should always trust
For he is our most important friend
Now as we search for tomorrow
To find our guiding light
We must understand if the price is
right

For some of us are bold
All of us are beautiful
So as the world turns
We must continue to learn
That we have one life to live
Still we must believe
That we are all God's children
And he shall be with us until the end

No Answer No Answer

My mind begins to wonder just what
is going on
So I pick up the phone just to give
you a call
No answer no answer
Now my mind begins to run wild and
I kinda stall
So I pick up the phone to give you
another call
No answer no answer
Frustration sets in I don't know what
to do
So I talk to some friends and wonder
if they knew
No answer no answer
My thoughts turn another way on
how I lived my past

So trouble in my way I sang that day Now I try my call again to see if it's the right number
But to no avail frustration sets in
No answer no answer

Hands of Time

*I wish I could turn back the hands of time
And start all over again
Know the things I know now
That I did not know back then
Like the things that fill your heart
with joy and laughter
And the things that make you smile
Like watching the sunrise on a clear day
And the moon shining on the bay
I wish I could turn back the hands of time
And start all over again
Know the things I know now
That I did not know back then*

I would pick you a rose from the garden
So early in the spring
Fix you breakfast each morning and
Dinner before you retire for bed
Kiss you right before I go to work
With a hug, it won't hurt
And let you know I love you
And you're always on my mind
I wish I could turn back the hands of time And start all over again
Know the things I know now
That I didn't know back then

Give me one more chance

Give me one more chance to love you To hold you in my arms
Give me one more chance to love you To enjoy your wonderful charm
Give me one more chance to love you To hold you in the night
Give me one more chance to love you To let you know things are alright Give me one more chance
To greet you with a kiss
Give me one more chance to love you To show you how you are never missed
Give me one more chance to love you To walk hand and hand
Give me one more chance to love you To love you like I have planned

Often

So often I think of you
Now let me tell you why
Sometimes I cant see you
And tears fall from my eyes
In a world so crazy
Theres many things we do
But in my world something is missing And what's missing is you
Continue to do as you do
And I pray you'll never fall
You're like an Angel in heaven
Who is always standing tall

Lift Me Up

Lift me up oh Lord today
Please show me your way
Lift me up on Lord right now
There's so much I need to say
Lift me up sad tears I've cried
And yes these tears are real
Lift me up from a world so troubled Teach me how to feel
Lift me up from all the sorrow
Please just lift me up tomorrow
Lift me up oh Lord today
Just show me your way

Teach me how not to fear the unseen
Teach me not to worry about what tomorrow brings
Teach me to look deep inside and to realize
Teach me of a mothers love that's sent from above
Teach me how you died, for all my sins Teach me

My Pain Within

*My Pain within runs so deep
When I sleep I often weep
My pain within it guides my way
Tomorrow I know will be a brighter day
My pain within I can't let go
My freedom is my greatest show
My pain within it gives me tears
Lord knows I been sick too many years
My pain within it gives me grace
To see that smile on my mama's face*

In My Deepest Thoughts

In My Deepest Thoughts you are always there
Your smile, your laughter, the way you care
A friendship that means so much I pray will never end
Seems it wasn't long ago and yes it will be again
I think of how we lived yesterday
Now today we found a better way
Thoughts of you keep a smile on my face
Yes you touched me in the right place
Now GOD has entered into our lives
To show us his way is the only way
I pray for you each day some days all day

For you to continue to stay strong and never go astray
The star's are there for you to reach Please keep me on your mind
Soon I'll be there once again
In My Deepest Thoughts

How Do We Begin to Understand

How do we begin to Understand
When understanding we've never known
The frustration, pain and stress
Things we try to ignore
How do we begin to understand
Where to find happiness
When happiness we think is just a dream
And happiness we never seen
How do we begin to understand
And win this troubled race
While in this race we do not know
Just what we might face
How do we begin to understand
And place our burdens behind us
For all of our lives deep inside
We so often hide them
How do we begin to understand

The other man
When all in their minds negativity
Has ruled our land
How do we begin to understand
Just how to live
When deep in our hearts we know
How do we begin to understand
And place our burdens behind us
For all of our lives deep inside
We so often hide them
How do we begin to understand
The other man
When all in their minds negativity
Has ruled our land
How do we begin to understand
Just how to live
When deep in our hearts we know
Not what to believe
How do we begin to understand
And not fear the unseen
When thoughts of terror in the night
Makes you want to scream
How do we begin to understand
And teach the world to love
Then convince them that gods love Is from above How do we begin to understand
To love all over again
Come together as a world
We should all be friends
How do we begin to understand
That God is on our side
For he has always been with us and it's time for us to win
How do we begin to understand
when understanding we have never known

On My Knees

On my knees today I prayed
For GOD to save my soul
On my knees today I prayed
So that I can be whole
On my knees today I pray
Because I seen mama pray this way
On my knees today I pray
Because I am awake today
On my knees today I prayed
For all the blessings GOD has given me
On my knees today I prayed
Because I give all glory to thee

No One Knew

No one knew my struggle
No one knew my pain
No one knew how I
Cried in the pouring rain
No one knew for years and years
Of my mothers tears
No one ever knew
Of my deepest fears
No one ever knew my struggle
No one ever knew my pain
No one knew how I lived
My life totally insane
No one ever knew
When my madness would end
Because no one knew
My struggle and no one knew my
pain

PART III

And then comes Recovery

Sick

Sick are the addicts
Who cant change their ways
For they can't see brighter days
Sick are the addicts
That has no will
and really can't be real
Sick are the addicts who cant say no and
May not know which way to go
Sick are the addicts that can't forgive
The ones who have yet learned to live
Sick are the addicts with those shifty eyes
The ones who have yet to realize
Sick are the addicts who think they're slick Sick are the addicts I'll never forget

The Perfect World

All the flowers are blooming with the skies so clear
You can hear the birds singing throughout the year
In this place you will know what love is about
The elders are always humming how great thou art
Every kid is playing with their little toys
Blessings are always here, it's such a joy
You can hear the happiness all in the air
Sorrow, sadness and pain will disappear
Every heart beats the same and everyone knows your name
Theres no madness and life isn't insane
All the streets are paved with natural gold
While the king sits high upon his throne
This is the perfect world that GOD hath made one day

To Be A Winner In Life

To be a winner in life
Is all I want to be
To be a winner in life
And a man in recovery
To be a winner in life
So I can smile again
To be a winner in life
And not have to live in sin
To be a winner in life
Cause I lost so much before
To be a winner in life
And there much more
To be a winner in life
And share my experience, strength and hope To be a winner in life
And guess what there is hope after dope
To Be a Winner in life

Sister Prayed and Mama Cried

Sister prayed and mama cried
For GOD to save my soul
So many years of addiction
Had deterred me from my goals
Sister prayed and mama cried
Now I realize the lifestyle I lived
In the past was not supposed to last
Sister prays today because she's so happy
That I have seen the light
Mama cries and is always elated
Because now I walk with that spiritual
light Sister Prayed and Mama Cried

Realize

Once addicted to a life
That was filled with alcohol and drugs Had some faith but no works
And realized life was no fun
Looked at the man in the mirror
And asked God to save his soul
Then he sent me to a fellowship
Now my life has begun
Now there is no trouble
Now I see the light
There's even peace in my heart
When I sleep at night
So look at that person in the mirror
Each day you rise
Because GOD gives us the strength
To live and realize

Free

*Free from yesterday because yesterday is gone
Not worried about tomorrow, I want to be alone
God will keep me safe as I pray each day
And guide me to a place and carry me along the way
Free from mankind and all his dislike
Soaring so free like a hawk in the night
Free from the unknown and things I don't know
Because GOD is the author and finisher I know
Free so free because I rose again
And I pray you'll be free
Because GOD is our friend*

Allow Us

Allow us to capture love
As we walk hand in hand and fulfill fantasies
As our hearts beat as one
Forever and forever
Just us
Keep our fire of love lit
As we love each other we wont forget
Holding each other
Oh so close each day
Unconditional love
Is the only way
Candle light dinners
And rose petal baths
I'll tell you I love you
You wont have to ask
Together our love
It's our most precious gift
The caring and sharing

Will keep us convinced
How can we go wrong
When our love is so strong
Loving each other
We will never be alone
Let's dance to slow music
All through the night
Today in our life
God has shown his light

Fellowship

*The Fellowship has shown me things
I've never seen before
The fellowship has taught me
things Now I always go back for
more
The fellowship I listen well and
Never do I dwell
on those past behaviors
That had me living in hell
The fellowship is a place that
Will help you smile again
The fellowship is a place
Which you will love until the end*

GOD'S way

God's way is the only way
Now I see that today
The years have past
still I lasted
Through all those troubled days
I tried it my way
But that wasn't right
Now I truly see the light
A spiritual man I am today
Because I'm doing it GOD'S way

It's Not the Same

It's not the same no more
The way I live my life today
It's not the same no more
But I still pray
It's not the same no more
For this addicted man
It's not the same no more
I'm in GOD'S hand
It's not the same no more
However it's better
Because it's not the same no more

He Gives me Strength

He gives me strength each day I rise
And everyday I smile
He gives me strength for all those sick days Now I've changed those times
He gives me strength and lifts me up
His love I do adore
He gives me strength to walk again
And live my life some more
He gives me strength and tells me why
Life is easy when you try
He gives me strength and this I know
He is the author and finisher of my show

www.ingramcontent.com/pod-product-compliance
Lightning Source LLC
Chambersburg PA
CBHW072106290426
44110CB00014B/1855